The Paleo Gourmet:

Delicious Paleo Dessert Recipes for the Paleo Diet

By Grace Minello

Disclaimer

The information herein is offered for informational purposes solely, and is universal as so. The presentation of the information is without contract or any type of guarantee assurance.

The trademarks that are used are without any consent, and the publication of the trademark is without permission or backing by the trademark owner. All trademarks and brands within this book are for clarifying purposes only and are the owned by the owners themselves, not affiliated with this document.

Table of Contents

Introduction

I want to thank you for downloading my book, *"The Paleo Gourmet: Delicious Paleo Dessert Recipes for the Paleo Diet"*.

Basically, Paleo is the short word for Paleolithic Diet. It is a way of eating that mimics the eating habits of cavemen—which means, you have to say good bye to your candies, cereal, chips and pasta and see more of seeds, vegetables, leafy greens, nuts, and wild fish and game on your plates.

However, being on a Paleo Diet does not mean that you cannot enjoy good deserts and gourmet tasting food. It's just all about picking the types of food in your diet that are not included in any caveman's diet. Take for example, potato chips—that wasn't a food staple back then. What our ancestors do to get food was to hunt game and gather food to eat.

So, now I want to introduce you to Paleo Diet Desert recipes that you can enjoy over and over again, without counting calories and still achieve your weight loss goals.

Thanks again for downloading this book, I hope you enjoy it!

Chapter 1: Justifying Your Sweet Tooth

Let's face it, majority of deserts are made from sugars—and that's what makes it sweet and lovable to a person. Now, the question is, was there sugar already during the Paleolithic era? What about grains? Aren't cakes, cookies and the likes are usually made of grains? Yes, they sure are and definitely, if there were grains in the Paleolithic times, it's not as abundant as what we have now. And definitely, they don't have grains in powdered form. So, does this all mean that having a piece of Paleo diet approved dessert is impossible?

Don't fret because we have found ways to satisfy your sweet tooth while still following the Paleo Diet strategy properly. But I need to remind you that you need to skimp on the dessert and just treat yourself to an occasional weekly dose of dessert aside from fruit portions. To help you, I have outline below several tips to beat a craving.

1 – Prevent Your Cravings

How? Simple. Do not skimp on your dose of carbs. Do not forget to add Paleo-friendly starchy foods in your diet to prevent your craving of junk foods. Another way to beat cravings is to eat when you are hungry. Once your stomach starts to growl, it means you are hungry and it's not just some food craving. So, feed your grumbling stomach with high quality protein and fat.

2 – Distract Yourself

Sometimes, when we have too much time on our hands all we ever think about is food. So, I suggest that you keep yourself busy to keep your mind off of food. You can do things like: taking a nap, clean your home, clean your car, call a friend, read a book and others.

3 – Work it Out

Most of all, if you are really on a diet to lose weight do not forget to workout. At least 30 minutes a day of rigorous exercise is advised. Working out will also curb your food cravings knowing how much effort you have put in to lose weight—definitely you will be mindful of your food intake.

So, without further ado, I am presenting to you 25 different Paleo Diet Dessert recipes to enjoy.

Chapter 2: Paleo Diet Dessert Recipes

1) Chocolate-Coconut Paleo Bars

Number of Servings: 12
Calories per Serving: 99.5 calories
Cholesterol: 0 mg
Fiber: 1.4 g
Sodium: 1.5 mg
Carbohydrates: 3.9 g
Fat: 9.8 g
Protein: 1.3 g

Ingredients:
1 tbsp honey
¾ cup shredded coconut, unsweetened
½ cup ground nuts (almonds, pecans, or walnuts)
¼ cup unsweetened cocoa powder
4 tbsps coconut oil

Directions:

1) In a medium bowl, mix shredded coconut, nuts and cocoa powder.
2) Add honey and coconut oil.
3) Mix batter thoroughly.
4) In a 9x9 square inch pan or dish, press the batter and for 30 minutes place in the freezer.
5) Evenly cut into 12 pieces, serve and enjoy.

2) *Zuchini, Banana, Chocolate-Almond Paleo Bread*

Number of Servings: 8
Calories per Serving: 85 calories
Cholesterol: 41.1 mg
Fiber: 1.8 g
Sodium: 78 mg
Carbohydrates: 7.1 g
Fat: 5.8 g
Protein: 3.1 g

Ingredients:
1 tsp baking powder
2 pcs Ghirardelli Midnight Reverie 86% Cocoa
1 tsp honey
1 tsp ground cinnamon
2 medium fresh eggs
1 cup grated zucchini
1 small fresh banana
½ cup ground almonds

Directions:

1) Grease a bread pan and preheat oven to 350ºF.
2) Mix thoroughly all ingredients in a medium bowl.
3) Transfer batter to greased bread pan and pop into the oven and bake until tops are golden brown around 30-35 minutes.
4) Remove from oven and let cool for 5-10 minutes, slice into 8 equal pieces.
5) Serve and enjoy while warm.

3) Chocolate Paleo Quickie Cake

Number of Servings: 1
Calories per Serving: 300.1 calories
Cholesterol: 286.8 mg
Fiber: 1.8 g
Sodium: 339.1 mg
Carbohydrates: 12.4 g
Fat: 29.2 g
Protein: 9 g

Ingredients:
2 tbsps heavy whipping cream
2 tsps Truvia
1 tbsp Butter
½ tsp Baking powder
1 tbsps unsweetened cocoa powder
1 extra large egg

Directions:

1) In a small microwave safe bowl, melt butter in microwave.
2) Beat in egg and whisk well.
3) Add all the dry ingredients and continue whisking until smooth and well blended.
4) Pop into microwave and cook on high for 45 seconds. If still not cooked, add 15 seconds more.
5) Pierce cake with fork and add the whipping cream.
6) Enjoy while hot!

4) Chocolate Chip Cookies Paleo Style

Number of Servings: 32
Calories per Serving: 136.2 calories
Cholesterol: 11.6 mg
Fiber: 1.5 g
Sodium: 117.9 mg
Carbohydrates: 10.1 g
Fat: 10.6 g
Protein: 2.6 g

Ingredients:
1 ½ cups chocolate chips
1 tsp vanilla extract
1 tsp salt
1 tsp baking soda
2 eggs
½ cup pure maple syrup
½ cup coconut oil
3 cups almond flour

Directions:

1) Ready a baking sheet and line it with parchment paper while preheating oven to 375ºF.
2) In a medium bowl, whisk together all dry ingredients.
3) In another bowl, whisk vanilla, syrup and eggs thoroughly before pouring into bowl of dry ingredients and mixing well to incorporate.
4) In a microwave safe bowl, melt coconut oil and pour into batter. Mix well.
5) Add chips, mix well.
6) Scoop 1 tbsp of cookie dough and drop into lined baking sheet at least 1.5 inch apart.
7) Pop into the oven and bake until lightly browned around 12-15 minutes.

5) Chocolate Balls Paleo Style

Number of Servings: 15
Calories per Serving: 63.3 calories
Cholesterol: 0
Fiber: 1.9 g
Sodium: 0.6 mg
Carbohydrates: 14.2 g
Fat: 1.3 g
Protein: 0.9 g

Ingredients:
¼ tsp vanilla, optional
3 tbsps unsweetened cocoa
3 tbsps walnuts
1 cup dates

Directions:

1) In a food processor, grind the dates. Once done, transfer to a medium mixing bowl.
2) Next, grind the walnuts in food processor to your desired fineness. Transfer into mixing bowl where the dates are.
3) Add remaining ingredients into mixing bowl and mix until smooth.
4) Roll batter into fifteen equal sized balls.

6) Chocolate Chip-Banana Paleo Muffins

Number of Servings: 11
Calories per Serving: 404.5 g
Cholesterol: 100.9 mg
Fiber: 5.5 g
Sodium: 46.8 mg
Carbohydrates: 20.8 g
Fat: 35.2 g
Protein: 6.4 g

Ingredients:
½ cup chocolate chips
½ cup coconut flour
½ tsp salt
½ tsp nutmeg
¼ cup melted coconut oil
6 eggs
½ tsp baking soda
3 mashed over ripe bananas

Directions:

1) Line muffin tins with baking cups and preheat oven to 350°F.
2) In a large baking bowl mix thoroughly melted coconut oil, mashed bananas, nutmeg, salt, baking soda and eggs.
3) Mix in flour and whisk until smooth.
4) Add chocolate chips and whisk until just incorporated.
5) With a level ice cream scoop, scoop batter evenly into prepared muffin tins.
6) Pop in the oven and bake until lightly browned or around 25-30 minutes.
7) Remove from oven, allow to cool, serve and enjoy.

7) Chunky Dark Chocolate Paleo Cookies

Number of Servings: 15
Calories per Serving: 124.4 calories
Cholesterol: 0
Fiber: 1.7 g
Sodium: 44.8 mg
Carbohydrates: 5.9 g
Fat: 10.6 g
Protein: 2.5 g

Ingredients:
½ of Dark Chocolate Lover's Chocolate Bar Trader Koe's 85% cacao, broken into small chunks
1 tsp Kirkland pure vanilla extract
¼ tsp Baking soda
¼ tsp salt
¼ cup Agave Nectar
2 tbsps coconut oil
2 tbsps almond oil
1 ¼ cups almond flour

Directions:

1) Prepare cookie sheets by spraying with cooking spray and preheating oven to 325°F.
2) In a medium bowl, whisk together all dry ingredients. In a separate bowl, mix all wet ingredients.
3) Pour wet ingredients into bowl of dry ingredients and mix well.
4) Evenly make 15 cookie balls and place on cookie sheets at least 1.5-inches apart.
5) Pop in the oven and bake until done when they look barely doughy around 8-16 minutes.
6) Remove from pan and cool on a wire rack before eating.

8) Chewy Style Chocolate Chip Paleo Cookies

Number of Servings: 25
Calories per Serving: 157.8 calories
Cholesterol: 33.6 mg
Fiber: 3.1 g
Sodium: 140.6 mg
Carbohydrates: 7.7 g
Fat: 13.8 g
Protein: 4.4 g

Ingredients:
2 eggs
10 tbsps melted butter
1 ½ tbsps vanilla extract
1 tbsp agave nectar
½ cup Palm coconut crystals
½ cup dark chocolate chips
1 tsp baking soda
½ tsp sea salt
½ cup coconut flour
½ cup golden flaxseed meal
1 ½ cups almond flour

Directions:

1) Grease baking sheet and preheat oven to 350ºF.
2) Mix together all dry ingredients in a big bowl.
3) In a separate medium bowl, mix thoroughly eggs, vanilla, agave, sugar and melted butter.
4) Pour wet ingredients into the bowl of dry ingredients and mix thoroughly.
5) Mix in chips.
6) Evenly divide dough into 25 circles and place on greased cookie sheet.

7) Pop into the oven and cook until lightly browned or around 12-20 minutes.
8) Remove from pan, cool on a wire rack and then store or serve once cooled.

9) Chocolate Smoothie Paleo Style

Number of Servings: 2 24-oz smoothie
Calories per Serving: 558.9 calories
Cholesterol: 60 mg
Fiber: 8.6 g
Sodium: 283.4 mg
Carbohydrates: 68.9 g
Fat: 21.7 g
Protein: 27.6 g

Ingredients:
4 tbsps almond butter
2 cups almond milk
1 tbsp honey
2 medium bananas2 servings Whey protein powder
1 cup Spinach

Directions:

1) In a food processor, add all ingredients and pulse to desired smoothness.
2) You can add a few ice cubes and continue processing or place the processed smoothie in the freezer for ten minutes before enjoying.
3) Evenly divide the smoothie into two glasses, serve and enjoy.

10) Chocolate Paleo Pudding

Number of Servings: 4
Calories per Serving: 359.5 calories
Cholesterol: 0
Fiber: 9.5 g
Sodium: 11 mg
Carbohydrates: 48.4 g
Fat: 21.6 g
Protein: 3.9 g

Ingredients:
1 tsp vanilla extract
1 tbsp coconut oil
½ cup raw honey
½ cup cocoa powder
2 ripe avocadoes

Directions:

1) In a food processor, process all ingredients until smooth.
2) Evenly divide into 4 bowls and put in the ref for an hour to cool and set before serving.

11) Paleo Friendly Raspberry-Chocolate Dessert

Number of Servings: 4
Calories per Serving: 133.1 calories
Cholesterol: 92.5 mg
Fiber: 5.1 g
Sodium: 38.8 mg
Carbohydrates: 7.5 g
Fat: 9.5 g
Protein: 4.8 g

Ingredients:
1 cup canned coconut milk
1 tsp vanilla extract
2 eggs
6oz 70% cacao or higher chocolate, chopped into bite sized pieces

Directions:

1) In a high speed food processor, blend vanilla, eggs and chocolate pieces.
2) In a microwave oven safe bowl, heat coconut milk until steaming but not boiling, around one to two minutes.
3) While whisking vigorously, whisk in coconut milk into egg-chocolate mixture. The heat from the blender and coconut milk will cook the eggs.
4) In 4 ramekins, evenly divide raspberries, pour custard mixture, cover and put in the ref for two hours.
5) Top with chocolate shavings and extra raspberries.

12) Pumpkin-Chocolate Paleo Muffins

Number of Servings: 10
Calories per Serving: 184.1 calories
Cholesterol: 0.1 mg
Fiber: 5.1 g
Sodium: 38.6 mg
Carbohydrates: 13 g
Fat: 14.8 g
Protein: 5.8 g

Ingredients:
2 packets Truvia – optional
1 tsp cinnamon
1 tsp vanilla extract
½ tsp baking powder
½ cup baking cocoa
1 cup canned pumpkin
3 tbsps almond butter
1 ¼ cups almond flour

Directions:

1) Mix all ingredients thoroughly in a medium bowl.
2) Evenly divide ingredients in ten muffin tins lined with baking cups.
3) Pop in the oven and bake for 20-25 minutes on a preheated 350ºF oven.
4) Remove from oven and tin, let it cool before serving.

13) Chocolate Banana Paleo Bread

Number of Servings: 9
Calories per Serving: 360.6 calories
Cholesterol: 41.1 mg
Fiber: 4 g
Sodium: 217.6 mg
Carbohydrates: 21.8 g
Fat: 29.2 g
Protein: 7.1 g

Ingredients:
1 tsp vanilla
1 cup chopped walnuts, optional
¼ cup melted chocolate, optional
1 tsp baking soda
1 tsp baking powder
2 eggs
3 medium brown, spotty bananas
1 cup almond flour
1 cup almond butter

Directions:

1) Grease a loaf pan and preheat oven to 350ºF.
2) Mix thoroughly all ingredients except for the chocolate.
3) Pour batter into loaf pan and top with chocolates.
4) Pop into the oven and bake until center is firm to touch or around 35-40 minutes.
5) Remove from oven and let it cool.
6) Evenly slice into 9 pieces, serve and enjoy.

14) Paleo Watermelon Fruity Bowl

Number of Servings: 16
Calories per Serving: 201 calories
Cholesterol: --
Fiber: 2.4 g
Sodium: 10 mg
Carbohydrates: 34.5 g
Fat: 7.2 g
Protein: 3.6 g

Ingredients:
¼ cup blueberries
1 serving cover honey
1 tsp vanilla extract
4 oz almonds, dry roasted
½ cup blackberries
10 raspberries
1 cup canned coconut cream
1 15 x 7 inch watermelon

Directions:

1) Cut ½-inch off the bottom of the watermelon to make it stable enough to stand on its own.
2) Cut off 1/3 portion of the watermelon and scoop out its flesh to carve it into a cylinder. Freeze watermelon flesh for 20-30 minutes.
3) Meanwhile in a small bowl, whip vanilla, honey and coconut cream.
4) Mix cream with frosted watermelon.
5) Arrange watermelon back into the watermelon bowl, garnish with the rest of nuts and berries.
6) Serve cold.

15) Pumpkin Custard Paleo Style

Number of Servings: 5
Calories per Serving: 60.5 calories
Cholesterol: 74 mg
Fiber: 1.6 g
Sodium: 65.5 mg
Carbohydrates: 4.4 g
Fat: 3.1 g
Protein: 5 g

Ingredients:
1 cup coconut milk
1 tsp vanilla extract
¼ cup stevia or less
2 egg whites
2 whole eggs
nutmeg to taste
pinch of sea salt
¼ tsp ground ginger
1 tsp cinnamon

Directions:

1) Bring a pot of water to boil while setting the oven to 350°F.
2) In a big bowl, mix all spices and pumpkin.
3) In a small bowl, whisk eggs and mix in vanilla, milk and sweetener.
4) Pour egg mixture into spice mixture and blend thoroughly.
5) Evenly divide mixture into 5 ramekins. Place ramekins on baking pan, pour the boiling water around them up to 2-inch of the ramekins, more than halfway.
6) Pop into the oven and bake until toothpick comes out clean when inserted, around 60 minutes.
7) You can enjoy the custard warm or cold.

16) Coffee Paleo Cake

Number of Servings: 9
Calories per Serving: 300.2 calories
Cholesterol: 36.2 mg
Fiber: 3.8 g
Sodium: 215.7 mg
Carbohydrates: 26.7 g
Fat: 20.8 g
Protein: 6.9 g

Ingredients:
½ tsp salt
½ tsp baking soda
½ cup arrowroot powder
2 cups almond flour
1 tsp vanilla
¼ cup raw local honey
2 eggs
½ cup coconut milk
¼ cup chopped walnuts

Directions:

1) Grease a 7 x 9 inch baking pan and preheat oven to 325ºF.
2) In a big bowl whisk all dry ingredients together except walnuts.
3) In a medium bowl, mix all wet ingredients together.
4) Pour wet ingredients into bowl of dry ingredients and mix well.
5) Pop into the oven and bake until a toothpick comes out clean or around 25-30 minutes.
6) Remove from oven, let cool before slicing into 9 equal slices.

17) *Avocado Chocolate Paleo Cake*

Number of Servings: 8
Calories per Serving: 450 calories
Cholesterol: 95 mg
Fiber: 8 g
Sodium: 140 mg
Carbohydrates: 49 g
Fat: 26 g
Protein: 12 g

Ingredients:
½ cup chocolate chips (optional)
4 large eggs
2 ripe, medium California Avocadoes, peeled, seeded and mashed
½ cup coconut palm sugar
½ cup dark honey
¼ tsp salt
½ tsp baking soda
2 cups finely ground almond flour
1 tbsp vanilla extract
½ cup boiling water
2/3 cup cocoa powder

Directions:

1) Line a loaf pan with baking paper and preheat oven to 325°F.
2) Whisk together cocoa powder, vanilla extract and boiling water in a small bowl.
3) Combine salt, baking powder, and sifted almond flour in a big bowl.
4) In a food processor process until smooth the avocadoes, coconut sugar and honey.
5) Pour chocolate mixture into food processor and continue processing until smooth.
6) Add eggs and pulse some more.

7) Pour mixture of the food processor into the big bowl of dry ingredients and mix thoroughly. Fold in choco chips if using.
8) Transfer batter into loaf pan, pop into the oven, and bake until knife comes out clean when inserted around 50 minutes.
9) Remove cake from oven, let cool for 20 minutes before slicing evenly into 8 slices.

18) Zucchini-Carrot Paleo Muffin

Number of Servings: 12
Calories per Serving: 203 calories
Cholesterol: --
Fiber: --
Sodium: --
Carbohydrates: 9 g
Fat: 16 g
Protein: 6 g

Ingredients:
1/8 cup of raisins – optional
½ tsp of sea salt
½ tsp of baking soda
1 ½ tsps of cinnamon
1 tsp vanilla extract
¼ cup melted organic coconut oil
¼ cup melted raw honey
¾ cup of grated zucchini, unpeeled
½ cup of grated carrots, peeled
1 tbsp of coconut flour
2 whisked eggs

Directions:

1) Prepare muffin tins by lining with baking paper and preheat oven to 350°F.
2) Mix sea salt, baking soda, cinnamon, coconut flour and almond flour in a big bowl.
3) In another bowl, combine well vanilla extract, organic coconut oil, raw honey and eggs.
4) Pour wet ingredients into the bowl of dry ingredients and mix well.
5) Add raisins, grated zucchini and carrots until thoroughly mixed.

6) Evenly divide the batter into the muffin tins and pop into the oven.
7) Bake muffins until tops are golden brown around 25-30 minutes.
8) Remove from oven and let cool before serving.

19) Strawberry Shortcake Paleo Style

Number of Servings: 8
Calories per Serving: 136 calories
Cholesterol: --
Fiber: --
Sodium: --
Carbohydrates: 12 g
Fat: 9 g
Protein: 4 g

Ingredients:
2 cups fresh strawberries, sliced
1 tbsp lemon juice
2 tbsps local honey
2 eggs
¼ tsp sea salt
1 tsp baking soda
3 cups almond flour

Coconut Whipped Cream Ingredients:
1 tsp vanilla extract
1 tbsp honey
1 can full fat coconut milk, refrigerated

Directions:

1) Line baking sheet with baking paper and preheat oven to 325ºF.
2) Whisk together lemon juice, honey and eggs in a small bowl.
3) Then mix salt, baking soda and almond flour in large bowl.
4) Pour in the wet ingredients into the large bowl and mix well.
5) Add 2 spoonful of batter into baking sheet and press down with back of spoon. Repeat until all batter is gone.
6) Pop into oven and bake until lightly browned around 15-20 minutes.

7) Meanwhile make the coconut whipped cream by whisking on high the vanilla, honey and coconut for 5 minutes.
8) Once shortcake is baked, let it cool, top with whipped coconut cream and fresh strawberries.

20) Paleo Ice Cream from Coconut Milk

Number of Servings: 4
Calories per Serving: 240 calories
Cholesterol: --
Fiber: --
Sodium: --
Carbohydrates: 16 g
Fat: 19 mg
Protein: 4 g

Ingredients:
Pinch of sea salt
Dash of cinnamon, optional
1-2 tsp vanilla extract
Ice cubes, if not using an ice cream maker
4 large dates, pitted
1 banana, frozen, if not using an ice cream maker
2 cans of organic full fat coconut milk, about one 13-oz can, chilled overnight

Directions:

1) Flip coconut milk can vertically on the opposite end it was standing in the ref. This will let you pour off the liquid part and leaving only the milk fat. Separate the liquid part from the milk fat part.
2) Use only the milk fat and the rest of the ingredients and put into a high speed food processor and process until creamy and thick.
3) Once done, chill for two to four hours before enjoying.

21) Orange and Date Paleo Shake

Number of Servings: 2
Calories per Serving: 486
Cholesterol: --
Fiber: --
Sodium: --
Carbohydrates: 69 g
Fat: 23 g
Protein: 9 g

Ingredients:
3 tsps water
20 g raisins
100 g cashews, not salted
100 g dates, pitted
1 large Orange

Directions:

1) Extract the juice and zest the orange.
2) Place all ingredients in the food processor and process until smooth.
3) Transfer into two glasses, serve and enjoy.

22) Lemon-Blueberry Paleo Pound Cake

Number of Servings: 8
Calories per Serving: 164 calories
Cholesterol: --
Fiber: 5 g
Sodium: --
Carbohydrates: 12 g
Fat: 10 g
Protein: 7 g

Ingredients:
1 ½ cups blueberries
¼ cup + 2 tbsps water
3 eggs
1 ½ tsps vanilla extract
1 ½ tsps lemon extract
1 ½ tsps baking powder
¼ tsp salt
¾ cup Splenda granulated
¼ cup + 2 tbsps coconut flour
1 cup + 2 tbsps almond flour

Directions:

1) Grease a loaf pan and preheat oven to 350ºF.
2) Mix thoroughly baking powder, salt, Splenda, coconut flour and almond flour in a big bowl.
3) Mix well water, eggs, vanilla extract, and lemon extract in a medium bowl.
4) Pour wet ingredients into the big bowl of dry ingredients and thoroughly mix.
5) Layer 1/3 of batter and 1/3 berries into loaf pan and repeat process until batter is used up.
6) Pop into the oven and bake until top is lightly browned around 35 minutes.

7) Let it cool before slicing into 8 equal servings.

23) Paleo Brownies Made of Sweet Potato

Number of Servings: 16
Calories per Serving: 112.6 calories
Cholesterol: 36.6 mg
Fiber: 1.8 g
Sodium: 46.0 mg
Carbohydrates: 14.5 g
Fat: 5.3 g
Protein: 2.2 g

Ingredients:
Pinch of salt
¼ tsp cinnamon
¼ tsp vanilla extract
¼ tsp baking powder
2 tbsps unsweetened cocoa powder
3 tbsps coconut flour
½ cup chocolate chips
1/3 cup raw honey
¼ cup virgin coconut oil, melted
3 eggs, whisked
1 sweet potato

Directions:

1) Cook the sweet potato until soft, you can boil, bake or microwave it. Meanwhile, preheat oven to 350°F and grease an 8 x 8 baking pan.
2) Once cooked, peel skin off and mash in a big bowl.
3) Add whisked eggs, vanilla, honey and coconut oil into big bowl and mix well.
4) Add choco chips, salt, cinnamon, baking powder, cocoa powder and coconut flour and mix well.
5) Pop into the oven and bake until done around 30-35 minutes.

6) Remove from oven, let it cool before slicing evenly into 16 slices.

24) Custard Fruit Paleo Tart

Number of Servings: 12
Calories per Serving: 211.4 calories
Cholesterol: 54.3 mg
Fiber: 2.8 g
Sodium: 148.4 mg
Carbohydrates: 9.3 g
Fat: 2.8 g
Protein: 6.8 g

Crust Ingredients:
1 egg
2 tbsps honey
¼ cup coconut oil
¼ tsp baking soda
½ tsp sea salt
2 cups almond flour

Custard ingredients:
1 tsp vanilla extract
3 eggs
13.5-oz coconut milk
2 bananas

Topping Ingredients:
1 cup sliced strawberries, or other fruits of choice

Directions:

1) To make the crust: Mix well baking soda, salt and almond flour in a big bowl.
2) Whisk well eggs, honey, and coconut oil in a medium bowl.
3) Stir in wet ingredients into the big bowl of dry ingredients and mix well.

4) Press dough into a greased tart pan 9-inche sin diameter and put aside.
5) To make custard: Place all ingredients in a food processor and process until smooth and creamy.
6) Meanwhile, preheat oven to 350°F.
7) Pour custard over crust and pop into oven for 35-40 minutes.
8) Remove from oven, let cool completely and place in the ref for at least 4 hours.
9) Before serving, top with your favorite fruits or fruits in season.

25) Raisin-Peach Paleo Pie

Number of Servings: 8
Calories per Serving: 203.1 calories
Cholesterol: 20.4 mg
Fiber: 3.9 g
Sodium: 8.6 mg
Carbohydrates: 14.1 g
Fat: 15.2 g
Protein: 6.2 g

Crust Ingredients:
1 ½ tbsps coconut oil
1 medium egg
2 cups ground almonds

Filling Ingredients:
0.32-oz Bob's red mill Tapioca flour
½ tsp ground cinnamon
¼ cup packed raisins
2 cups sliced fresh peaches

Directions:

1) Grease a 9-inch round pie plate and preheat oven to 350ºF.
2) Combine all crust ingredients and press ½ of dough around bottom of pie plate. Reserve the other half for crumbling later on.
3) Pop in the oven and bake crust around 8-10 minutes or until lightly browned.
4) Make the filling by combining all ingredients in a bowl and layer on top of baked crust, top with crumbled crust and return to oven.
5) Bake pie until set around 15 minutes.
6) Remove from oven, let cool for 15 minutes, evenly cut into 8 slices and serve.

Manufactured by Amazon.ca
Bolton, ON